Samuel Nain
Manuel Nain

Production and Inventory Management

Samuel Nain
Manuel Nain

Production and Inventory Management

ScienciaScripts

Imprint
Any brand names and product names mentioned in this book are subject to trademark, brand or patent protection and are trademarks or registered trademarks of their respective holders. The use of brand names, product names, common names, trade names, product descriptions etc. even without a particular marking in this work is in no way to be construed to mean that such names may be regarded as unrestricted in respect of trademark and brand protection legislation and could thus be used by anyone.

Cover image: www.ingimage.com

This book is a translation from the original published under ISBN 978-620-0-02049-9.

Publisher:
Sciencia Scripts
is a trademark of
Dodo Books Indian Ocean Ltd. and OmniScriptum S.R.L publishing group

120 High Road, East Finchley, London, N2 9ED, United Kingdom
Str. Armeneasca 28/1, office 1, Chisinau MD-2012, Republic of Moldova, Europe
Printed at: see last page
ISBN: 978-620-6-87487-4

SIEP/ENTERPRISE

SIEP is a comprehensive modular business management system with ERP features, which is designed to model and automate most processes in the company (finance, purchasing, sales, logistics, inventory, budget, production, payroll, accounting, etc.), this application was designed and produced entirely in the programming and development rooms of the company, concentrated and converted into a reference model that responds to the concerns and needs of small and medium enterprises, to meet the need and demand for the software. At present, the software architecture team, analysts and product developers, SIEP has become a powerful tool designed to minimise the complex problems of efficiently managing and directing a company, providing support to all levels of the organisation.

CHAPTER 1 INTRODUCTION

The basis of any commercial enterprise is the purchase and sale of goods or services; hence the importance of inventory management. This accounting management will allow the company to maintain control in a timely manner, as well as to know at the end of the accounting period a reliable statement of the economic situation of the company.

Inventory is the current asset items that are ready for sale, i.e. all goods held in a company's warehouse valued at acquisition cost, for sale or production activities.

By means of the following research work, some basic concepts of everything related to inventories in a company, methods, system and control will be presented.

Inventory is a primary part of many businesses. Essentially, inventory is the storage of products that are venerable to consumers in order to make a profit. In addition, in some cases, inventory also includes what the company uses to keep the business up and running, for example, the storage of cleaners is considered inventory for a business that focuses on the   cleaning business   .

There are different forms of inventory and any company can rely on one or more forms of inventory. First, we mention materials and components inventory: this type of inventory is the storage of the various parts for the manufacture of larger products. For example, an automobile manufacturer has wheels or foot brakes in its inventory, available for use when needed to add to a car - that is manufacturing. Similarly, a Web designer may have a variety of software applications that help create innovative Web sites. However, another example of materials and inventory components can be seen in a restaurant: food in restaurants have their own refrigerators and freezers to then cook and serve to their guests.

Another form of inventory that a company may hold is products that are ready for sale. For example, some companies purchase their products from manufacturers and stockpile them in their warehouses: such facilities will require warehouse management in inventory. These products are ready for sale immediately and do not require assembly; toys, household goods, furniture and office supplies are just a few of the many items that can be part of a ready-for-sale inventory   .

Whether a business is the storage of products for later use or the storage of parts that are later used in the creation of products, the company must always know what they have in their hands. If one does not know what one has, there is no way for the business to function properly. Mismanagement of funds, lost profits, and theft are some of the most common consequences of poor inventory management.

ERP systems are integrated economic management systems for companies. They are characterised by the fact that they are composed of different parts that are integrated into a single application. These parts are of different uses, e.g. production, sales, purchasing, logistics, accounting (of various types), project management, GIS (geographic information system), inventory and control.

From warehouses, orders, payroll, etc. We can define an ERP as the integration of all these parts. It is not correct to consider a simple invoicing programme as an ERP just because a company integrates only that part. This is the fundamental difference between an ERP and another management application. ERP integrates everything necessary for the operation of the company's business processes. We cannot talk about ERP when only one or a small part of the business processes is integrated. The very definition of ERP indicates the need for "Availability of all information to everyone all the time".

This type of solution will allow companies to stay ahead of the curve, succeed in the markets they develop and keep up with international companies technologically. It is a structured system that seeks to meet the demand for business management solutions allowing companies to unify the different areas of productivity of the same.

This Brochure presents the compilation of Publications presented on the website www.siep-enterprise.com, these publications represent in some way a reference of the best Business Consultancy to provide guidance for the implementation of Enterprise Resource Planning (ERP) Software.

HOW TO DO A SUCCESSFUL STOCKTAKING

Physical inventory taking consists of carrying out an orderly process of physical verification of goods, raw materials or finished products at a given date, in order to ensure their actual existence.

The results obtained from the inventory are compared with the physical verification in order to establish their conformity. Subsequently, any differences that may exist are clarified and investigated by the people in charge, and the necessary adjustments are made, as the case may be. This process must be carried out periodically, according to the company's internal policies. To facilitate this procedure, we list 5 practical tips to carry out this task effectively:

1. DEFINE DATES FOR INVENTORY TAKING.

Periodic counting of goods allows stock levels to be monitored without interrupting warehouse production hours.

Known as one of the most efficient inventory counting methods for retailers, periodic inventory can be conducted on a daily or weekly basis (usually before the shop opens) and can avoid having to do full inventory counts.

If you must conduct a full physical inventory count, you should schedule it in advance.

2. SECTORING THE INVENTORY.

Due to the complexity of the inventory taking process and the large number of items in it, it is advisable to divide the warehouse into groups or families, in order to facilitate the counting of the products.

3. ENSURE THAT THERE ARE NO INVENTORY MOVEMENTS.

It must be ensured that there are no inventory movements (entries, exits, production process, etc.) at the time of physical stocktaking, in order to avoid disparity of balances.

4. RELYING ON TECHNOLOGY.

5.

Traditionally, physical inventory counts are done with a pencil and paper. Staff would use a physical count sheet to record the products and reconcile the data in the system.

If you are using inventory management software, check whether it offers physical counting functions.

6. ANALYSIS OF THE RESULTS.

After taking the physical inventory, it is necessary to analyse the results in order to know the inventory differences (over or shortage) of the process and to make the appropriate decisions.

Some of the causes of inventory differences may be:
1. Error in the physical count.
2. Error in the transcription of data.
3. Error in the reception or dispatch of the goods in the warehouse.
4. Theft, among others.

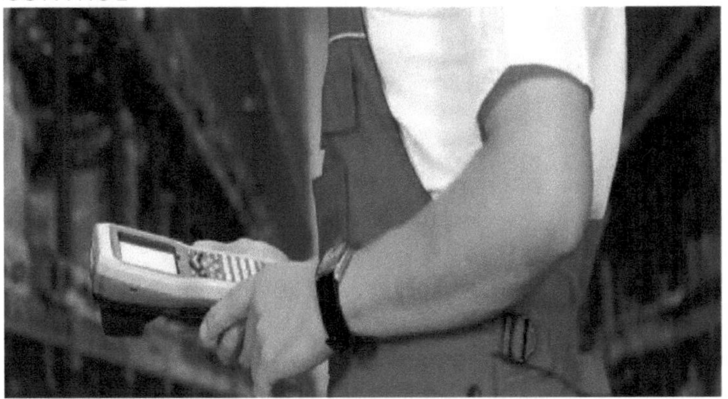

Inventory is the main organ of your company, i.e. the heart of your company, every flow or movement is reflected in it.

In order to achieve the sales targets set by the company, it is essential to maintain an adequate stock that allows it to fulfil all orders on time.

A good inventory control is the great ally to increase the profitability of your company, but even so, not all entrepreneurs are concerned about investing resources (economic, human, infrastructure) to optimise the stock and improve working conditions and end up affecting the company.

The most common mistakes that are made due to lack of proper inventory control:

Excess inventories: having overcrowded warehouses does not ensure high sales, it leads to lack of control, affects liquidity and above all harms companies that distribute perishable products. There is also the risk that the products will reach their expiry date, resulting in economic losses.

Insufficient inventories: on the other hand, keeping low levels of products in the warehouses results in a low response capacity when it comes to fulfilling orders and therefore runs the risk of generating a poor quality of service, resulting in customer dissatisfaction and increasing the likelihood that they will turn to competitors to satisfy their needs.

Lack of monitoring: When there is no record and history of both incoming and outgoing goods in the warehouses, there is no way to visualise the stock at any given time.

Losses due to Theft: When there is no control of the products, people may be tempted to engage in looting, generating new problems for the company with the corresponding economic consequences. Any tool that allows you to save and control your company's assets helps you to be more productive and generate more profit. Efficient inventory management is essential to ensure that the business has enough products in stock to meet consumer demand.

When competition is fierce, companies cannot afford to have money tied up in the form of goods in their inventory, nor can they afford to be unable to provide excellent customer service by running out of stock.

The aim is to achieve that balance between supply and demand, as well as to have reliability in the timing of receipt of goods from your supplier and delivery to your customers.

Having an Inventory Management System brings multiple advantages to your company by providing important and timely information in real time that will help you have a better planning and make the right decisions to be more efficient.

REMEMBER: To achieve these benefits for your company it is important to have the right technology to support you in managing your inventory in the most efficient way.

1. Establish best practices in the planning and execution of the whole process.
2. Establish rules for periodic review and monitoring.
3. Adequate and properly trained personnel.

Conclusion

By relying on an Inventory Management and Control System, your company will have an optimal stock management, which will generate an important competitive advantage by obtaining greater reliability in their stocks, as well as in costs and therefore better customer service to achieve the profitability you are looking for your company, plus all these advantages translate into economic benefits in the short and medium term.

The production budget is an estimate of the quantity of goods to be produced by the company over a given period of time. This requires converting the planned sales volume in terms of units to be produced as a basis for preparing budgets for the different aspects of the manufacturing activity.

The development of the production plan involves the adoption of policies related to achieving manufacturing stability and efficiency, better utilisation of manufacturing facilities and adequate levels of finished goods and work-in-process inventories.

This implies considering two specific types of problems:

1. Production planning
2. Inventory planning.

PRODUCTION PLANNING

In manufacturing enterprises it is necessary to establish in advance and in accordance with the sales budget, the volume of production to be achieved during the budgeted period. The production budget should be calculated for each product type and by department in terms of physical unit quantities.

The essential building blocks for developing an appropriate production plan are:

Establish the total production needs in terms of units of finished products.

1. Determine the working capacity of plant and equipment.
2. Study the need or not to increase the current capacity of the plant.
3. Establish the availability of raw materials and skilled manpower.
4. Examine the effect of the duration of the production process.

Total Production Requirements

The total production requirements are simply the conversion of the sales plan in terms of units to be produced, taking into account management's policies on finished goods inventories. Once the policies for finished goods inventories have been established and the annual production budget has been developed, the next step is to distribute it over interim periods throughout the year.

The sales budget, when broken down into quarters, months or weeks, reflects the seasonal behaviour of the market. The production budget may or may not be affected by these fluctuations; ultimately, it depends on the existing circumstances and the policy adopted by the management; in any case, its variations will not be similar to the variations in sales. A realistic sales budget should follow the expected peaks and troughs in sales volume throughout the year. The production budget will try to stabilise production at the same level, even if there is more than one level during the course of the year. The finished goods inventory covers the difference in behaviour between sales and the more or less stable production. This means that the inventory will inversely reflect the seasonal behaviour of sales.

Plant & Equipment Working Capacity

Production planning in a manufacturing enterprise requires consideration of the working capacity of available plant and equipment and of new fixed asset additions to be made, with a view to maintaining a proper balance between all manufacturing processes.

When talking about factory capacity, a distinction must be made between:

1. Maximum capacity.
2. Normal capacity.
3. Minimum capacity.

The maximum capacity of a factory to produce would be that achieved by running all the time without any limitation by delays and backlogs of any kind. From a practical point of view.

Normal capacity is between 75 % and 85 % of maximum capacity, taking into account the nature and circumstances of each plant and the efficiency of its operations. The ratio of normal capacity to maximum capacity allows the estimation of unused working capacity.

The minimum or break-even capacity is the one that must be achieved in order not to lose and depends on the minimum sales volume, at which the company neither gains nor loses. A thorough understanding of these aspects allows for better production planning and, therefore, cost reduction.

Increase in current production capacity

In close connection with the production budget and when analysing the current capacity of the factory, it is necessary to formulate the fixed asset investment budget or capital budget, with a view to meeting production requirements, upgrading current processes or developing new products.

Availability of raw materials and skilled labour

There is a close relationship between the volume of production and the availability of raw materials. Certain aspects related to the procurement of raw materials have to be carefully evaluated; among these, the perishable or non-perishable nature of the raw materials, the prices, the quality and the economic order quantity are worth mentioning. The availability of skilled labour and the time required for worker training have a decisive impact on production plans.

Duration of the manufacturing process

When formulating the production schedule, the influence of the duration of the manufacturing process on the production budget must be taken into account. If the duration of the manufacturing process is short, the sales budget is converted directly into the production budget. In situations where the manufacturing process is more or less time-consuming, it is necessary to draw up additional statements pointing out this special feature and the planned way to overcome it.

INVENTORY PLANNING

In production companies, inventories represent an important asset and at the same time have a decisive influence on aspects such as sales, production, purchasing and finance. Managers in different areas of the company have different views on the amount and availability of inventories.

Each of these affects inventories in a different way as explained below:

Sales: Finished goods inventory must be high in order to satisfy all market requirements promptly.

Production: Fluctuations in finished goods inventory should allow for a more or less stable production rate to be maintained. Adequate inventories of raw materials ensure a continuous flow in the manufacturing activity.

Purchasing: Procurement in adequate quantities of products needed for production reduces both the unit cost and the expenses related to purchasing management.

Finance: Reduced inventories reduce working capital requirements and the costs of maintaining them.

The above considerations reveal the conflict that exists in the inventory problem in companies. Excessive inventories cause operating, risk and investment costs that affect the company's performance and liquidity. Low inventories prevent the realisation of sales and production in harmony with market requirements and the company's production capacity.

The development of the production budget makes it necessary to consider the inventory problem in advance. As a starting point for tackling this problem, inventory policies should be expressed as precisely as possible.

There are several methods for developing and expressing a specific inventory policy. Among the most commonly used methods are the ceiling and floor method and the inventory turnover ratio method.

Minimum Inventory

It is defined as the amount of inventory below which it should not fall in order not to interfere with order fulfilment or the manufacturing process. The minimum inventory is established by taking into account customer or supplier habits, the usual size of orders, the possibility of occasional orders, etc. In addition, factors such as the duration of the manufacturing process and the time spent on transport, storage and delivery must be considered. If sales or purchases are highly seasonal, it may be necessary to set more than one minimum inventory limit.

Maximum inventory

It is defined as the amount of inventory that should not be exceeded in order to avoid excessive investments that disrupt the company's financial regime.

Inventory turnover

Inventory turnover ratios express the number of times finished goods, work-in-process or raw materials are moved in a year and converted into more liquid assets, such as cash or receivables.

Efficient inventory management is essential to ensure that the business has enough products in stock to meet consumer demand. Failure to manage it correctly can result in the business losing money on potential sales that cannot be fulfilled or wasting money by holding too much inventory. An inventory management system can prevent these types of mistakes from occurring.

When competition is fierce, companies cannot afford to have money tied up in the form of goods in their inventory, nor can they afford to be unable to provide excellent customer service by running out of stock.

The aim is to achieve that balance between supply and demand, as well as to have reliability in the timing of receipt of goods from your supplier and delivery to your customers.

Having an Inventory Management System brings multiple advantages to your company by providing important and timely information in real time that will help you to have a better planning and to make the right decisions to be more efficient.

Benefits of Managing your Inventory with SIEP:
Raw Material Management.
Finished Product Management.
Production Management
Management of Semi-processed Products (Products in Process).
Management of industrial leftovers.
Management of products for internal use (tools, spare parts, supplies).
Indirect Cost and Price Analysis, necessary to be able to establish profit margins on products in a reliable and secure way.
Management of incoming and outgoing products.
Stock Control and Danger Points for inventory replenishment.
Stock Management by Batch and Product Expiration Dates.
Analysis of Inventory Balances.
Ability to change prices in batches, quickly and reliably.
Warehouse and Production Line Management.

Real time information between Purchasing - Production - Warehouse - Sales - Dispatch - Administration and Accounting.
Integration with SIEP-ERP-Administrative and SIEP-ACCOUNTING

Remember that in order to achieve these benefits for your company it is important:

Having the right technology to support you in managing your inventory in the most efficient way.

Establish best practices in the planning and execution of the whole process.

Establish rules for periodic review and monitoring.

Adequate and properly trained personnel.

By relying on SIEP your company will have an optimal management of its inventories, which will generate an important competitive advantage by obtaining greater reliability in its stocks, as well as in costs and therefore a better customer service to achieve the profitability you are looking for your company.

Warehouse management involves a number of basic decisions:

A) Decide on the number of warehouses and their size.

B) Choosing locations for warehouses

C) The type and level of mechanisation. The first decision is whether to use owned, rented or third-party warehouses. Some products require specialised warehouses such as frozen products. Another fundamental decision is the level of automation of the warehouses. Nowadays we can have fully automated warehouses. Although sometimes an intermediate level of automation is more profitable.

D) Establish the organisation and specific management procedures.

E) The number of warehouses depends on several factors. A fundamental factor is the cost and duration of transport. A few years ago, transport in Europe was slower and there was some difficulty at borders. Improved communications and the elimination of borders within the European Union have made it easier to concentrate operations in fewer large automated warehouses.

Other key factors relate to product and market characteristics.

F) The location of the warehouses is decided by analysing the costs of the various alternative sites. And having as a fundamental constraint the maximum response time to customer orders.

G) Establish the organisational system. It is necessary to decide on the number of warehouse employees, select them, train them and assign them responsibilities. An important aspect in warehouses is the layout. That is, how the different products are distributed over the surface area of the warehouse.

For example, if we place the products with the greatest movement close to the exit, we reduce the total displacements.

Within the warehouse, it will be necessary to determine how the products, information and people or mechanical means will be moved. The different stages or tasks that will be carried out from the reception of the products in the warehouse until they leave.

We will have to precisely define the procedures. In other words, how the work will be carried out. Establish the different tasks of each process and how they are carried out.

. Basic Concepts

These are the places where different types of goods are stored.

The formulation of an inventory policy for a warehouse department depends on information regarding lead times, material availabilities, price trends and purchasing materials is the best source of this information.

This function physically controls and maintains all inventoried items, adequate physical safeguards must be established to protect the items from damage from unnecessary use due to faulty stock rotation procedures, faulty stock rotation procedures and theft. Records should be maintained, which facilitate the immediate location of items.

The role of warehouses:

A. They keep raw materials safe from fire, theft and damage.
B. Allow authorised persons access to the stored materials.
C. They keep the purchasing department constantly informed about the actual stock of raw materials.

D. Keeps meticulous controls on raw materials (inputs and outputs)
E. Ensure that materials are not used up (maxima - minima).
F. Stock function:
G. Secure supply and invalidates the effects of:
H. Delays in the supply of materials.
I. partial supply
J. Purchase or production in economic totals.
K. Speed and efficiency in meeting needs.

WAREHOUSE EQUIPMENT

Strategies and boxes:

The overall efficiency and flexibility of storage procedures can be greatly increased through the use of appropriate equipment. In some companies, the storage department constitutes the shelving, lockers, compartments, etc., which are made of ordinary wood and veneer. However, steel shelving has become more commonly used than wood shelving and can be purchased from specialised manufacturers in a wide variety of models and sizes.

RECEPTION FUNCTION:

The receiving function, whether from a company unit or a common carrier, is the same. If the material is received from any other source or other department of the company's construction activities, the procedure will be the same.

Importance:

The proper receiving of materials and other items is of vital importance, as a large part of the companies have as a result of their centralised experience the total receiving under a single department, the main exceptions being those large companies with multiple plants. Receiving is closely linked to purchasing, as probably 70% of the cases, the department under the responsibility of the purchasing department.

PROCESS

- Upon receipt of a shipment: It will be checked to see if it is in order and in good condition, if the container is damaged or if the required number of packages was not received. A corresponding caveat must be made immediately and no receipt of conformity can be given for the shipment, this is essential regardless of whether the transport is by air, sea or land, as it may be required to give <u>force</u> to any resulting claim for concealed shipments.

- Similarly: Material received by a company facility should also be subjected to a preliminary inspection before being introduced into the storage area, in the event that the initial inspection detects substandard material or material in poor condition, it should be rejected.

MATERIAL STORAGE TECHNIQUES

The storage of materials depends on the size and characteristics of the materials. These may require simple shelving to complicated systems, involving large investments and complex technologies. The choice of material storage system depends on the following factors:

- Space available for storage of materials.

- Types of materials to be stored.

- Types of materials to be stored.

- Number of items stored.

- Speed of attention needed.

- Type of packaging.

The chosen storage system must respect some essential MA techniques. The main material storage techniques are:

- Unit load: A unit load is a load consisting of transport packaging which arranges or packages a certain quantity of material so as to enable it to be handled, transported and stored as a unit. A unit load is a cargo contained in a container which forms a single whole for handling, storage or transport. The formation of unit boxes is done by means of a slide called a pallet, which is a schematic wooden pallet of various dimensions. Its basic conventional dimensions are 1100mm x 1100mm as an international standard to suit various means of transport and storage. Pallets can be classified as follows:

As for the number of entries in: 2 and 4 entry platforms.

2-inlet platform: used when the material movement system does not require the use of material handling equipment.

4-input platform: These are used when the material movement system requires the use of shunting equipment.

Boxes or crates. This is the ideal storage technique for small-sized materials, such as screws, rings or some office materials, such as pens, pencils, among others. Some materials that are being processed or semi-finished can be stored in boxes in the production sections themselves. The boxes or crates can be made of metal, wood or plastic. The dimensions must be schematized and their size can vary enormously. They can be built by the company itself or purchased from the supplier market.

Shelving: This is a storage technique for materials of various sizes and for the support of standardised crates and boxes. The shelves can be made of wood or metal profiles, of various sizes and dimensions, the materials stored in them must be identified and visible, shelving is the simplest and most economical means of storage. It is the technique adopted for small and light parts when stocks are not very large.

Columns: Columns are used to accommodate long and narrow pieces such as tubes, bars, straps, thick rods, straps among others. They can be mounted on casters to facilitate their movement, their structure can be made of wood or steel.

- Stacking: This is a variation of box storage to make maximum use of vertical space. The boxes or pallets are stacked one on top of the other, obeying an equal distribution of loads, it is a storage technique that reduces the need for divisions in the racks, since in practice, it forms a large single shelf. Stacking favours the use of platforms and consequently of stacks, which constitute the ideal equipment for moving them. It is the configuration of the stacking that defines the number of entrances required to the pallets.

- Flexible containers: One of the most recent storage techniques, the flexible container is a kind of sack made of strong fabric and vulcanised rubber, with an internal lining that varies according to its use. It is used for the storage and movement of bulk solids and liquids, with a capacity that can vary from 500 to 1000 kilos. It can be moved by means of stackers or cranes.

It is very common to use storage techniques associated with the stacking system of boxes or platforms, which provide flexibility and better vertical utilisation of the warehouses.

Physical Inventory

Inventory of goods is the verification or confirmation of the existence of the materials or assets of the company. In reality, the inventory is a physical statistic or count of the existing materials, in order to compare it with the existence recorded in the stock files or in the materials database.

Some companies call it physical inventory because it is a physical or palpable statistic of what is in stock in the company and to differentiate it from the stock recorded in the FE.

The physical inventory is carried out periodically, almost always at the end of the company's fiscal period, for the purpose of the accounting balance. On that occasion, the inventory is taken throughout the company; in the warehouse, in the sections, in the warehouse, among others. The physical inventory is important for the following reasons:

- Allows to verify differences between stock records in the FE and physical stock (actual stock quantity).

- It allows to verify the differences between the physical book stocks, in monetary values.

- Provides the approximation of the total value of (book) stocks, for balance sheet purposes, when the inventory is taken close to the end of the fiscal year.

The need for physical inventory is based on two reasons:

- The physical inventory complies with tax requirements, as they must be transcribed in the inventory book, in accordance with the legislation.

- The physical inventory satisfies the accounting need to verify, in reality, the existence of the material and the approximation of the actual consumption.

Materials Coding

To make it easier to locate the materials stored in the warehouse, companies use material coding systems. When the quantity of items is very large, it becomes almost impossible to identify them by their respective names, brands, sizes, etc.

To facilitate the management of materials, items must be classified on the basis of a rational system that allows for adequate storage procedures, warehouse operations and efficient stock control. The cataloguing, simplification, specification, standardisation, standardisation, schematisation and codification of all the materials that make up the company's stock is called item classification. Let us take a closer look at the concept of classification by defining each of its stages.

Cataloguing: Means an inventory of all existing items without omitting any. Cataloguing allows the presentation of all items together providing an overview of the collection.

Simplification: means the reduction of the great diversity of items used for the same purpose, when there are two or more parts for the same purpose, simplification is recommended in favour of standardisation.

Specification: means the detailed description of an item, such as its measurements, format, size, weight, etc. The higher the specification, the more information you will have about the item and the less uncertainty you will have about its composition and characteristics. The specification facilitates the purchasing of the item, as it gives the supplier a precise idea of the material to be purchased. It facilitates inspection on receipt of the material, product engineering work, etc.

Standardisation: Indicates the way in which the material should be used in its various applications. The word derives from standards, which are prescriptions on the use of materials.

Standardisation: means setting identical weight, size and format standards for materials so that there are not many variations between them. Standardisation means, for example, that screws are of such and such a specification, thus avoiding hundreds of different screws being unnecessarily stocked.

Thus, cataloguing, simplification, specification, normalisation and standardisation are the different steps towards classification. From classification, the materials can be coded.
CLASSIFICATION

    A. Cataloguing
    B. Simplification
    C. Specification
    D. Standardisation
    E. Standardisation

CODING

Classification and Coding of Materials

Thus, to classify a material is to group it according to its dimension, shape, weight, type, characteristics, use, etc. The classification must be done in such a way that each type of material occupies a specific place, which facilitates its identification and location in the warehouse.

Coding is a consequence of the classification of items. Coding means to represent each item by means of a code that contains the necessary and sufficient information, by means of numbers and letters. The most commonly used coding systems are: alphabetical, numerical and alphanumerical codes.

The alphabetical system codes materials with a set of letters, each of which identifies certain characteristics and specification. The alphanumeric system limits the number of items and is difficult to memorise, which is why it is rarely used.

The alphanumeric system is a combination of letters and numbers and6 covers a larger number of items. The letters represent the type of material and its group in this class, while the numbers represent the indicator code of the item.

Accounting for inventories is a very important part of merchandise accounting systems because the sale of inventory is the heart of the business. Inventory is usually the largest asset on your balance sheet, and inventory expenses, called cost of goods sold, are usually the largest expense on the income statement.

Companies dedicated to the purchase and sale of goods, as this is their main function and the one that will give rise to all other operations, will need constant summarised and analysed information on their inventories, which makes it necessary to open a series of main and auxiliary accounts related to these controls. These accounts include the following:

- Inventory (initial)

- Shopping

- Returns on purchase

- Purchasing costs

- Sales

- Sales returns

- Goods in transit

- Consignment goods

- Inventory (ending)

Opening Inventory represents the value of the stock of goods at the beginning of the accounting period. This account is opened when inventory control in the General Ledger is carried out on a speculative basis, and does not move again until the end of the accounting period when it will be closed either as a charge to cost of sales or directly to Profit and Loss.

The Purchases account includes goods purchased during the accounting period for the purpose of resale at a profit and which form part of the purpose for which the enterprise was created. Purchases of land, machinery, buildings, equipment, installations, etc. are not included in this account. This account has a debit balance, does not enter in the company's balance sheet, and is closed by Profit and Loss or Cost of Sales.

Returns on purchase, refers to the account that is created in order to reflect all purchased goods that the company returns for any reason; although this account will decrease the purchase of goods, it will not be credited to the purchases account.

Expenses incurred on purchases of goods should be directed to the account entitled: Purchasing Expenses. This account has a debit balance and is not included in the balance sheet.

Sales: This account will control all sales of goods made by the Company and which were purchased for this purpose. On the other hand we also have Returns on Sale, which is created to reflect the returns made by customers to the company.

On some occasions, especially if the company makes purchases abroad, we find that certain disbursements have been made or payment commitments (documents or drafts) have been acquired for goods that the company purchased but which, for reasons of distance or any other circumstance, have not yet been received at the warehouse. To account for this type of transaction, the account Goods in Transit should be used.

On the other hand, we have the account called Goods on Consignment, which is nothing more than the account that will reflect the goods that have been acquired by the company on "consignment", over which the company does not have any ownership rights, therefore, the company is not obliged to cancel them until they have been sold.

The Current (Ending) Inventory is taken at the end of the accounting period and corresponds to the physical inventory of the company's merchandise and its corresponding valuation. By relating this inventory with the initial one, with the net purchases and sales of the period, the Gross Profit or Loss in Sales of that period will be obtained.

The internal control of inventories starts with the establishment of a purchasing department, which should manage the purchasing of inventories following the purchasing process.

Inventory Systems

The Perpetual Inventory System:

In the Perpetual Inventory system, the business keeps a continuous record for each inventory item. The records therefore show the inventory on hand at all times. Perpetual records are useful for preparing financial statements on a monthly, quarterly or interim basis. The business can determine the cost of ending inventory and the cost of goods sold directly from the accounts without having to account for the inventory.

The perpetual system offers a high degree of control because inventory records are always up to date. Previously, businesses used the perpetual system mainly for high unit cost inventories, such as jewellery and automobiles; today, with this method, managers can make better decisions about quantities to purchase, prices to pay for inventory, customer pricing, and terms of sale to offer. Knowledge of the quantity on hand helps to protect inventory.

The derivation of the balance of each account includes the inventory:

Opening Balance

+ Increases (Purchases)

- Decreases in cost of goods sold

= Ending Balance

The balance of the inventory account under the perpetual system should result in the cost of inventory on hand at any point in time.

Perpetual inventory records provide information for the following decisions:

- Most furniture shops keep their merchandise in their warehouses, so employees cannot visually inspect the available merchandise and give an instant response. The perpetual system will indicate the availability of the merchandise in a timely manner.

- Perpetual records alert the business to reorganise inventory when it is low.

- If companies prepare financial statements on a monthly basis, perpetual inventory records show the existing ending inventory, no physical count is necessary at this time; however, a physical count is necessary once a year to verify the accuracy of the records.

Seats Under The Perpetual System

In the perpetual inventory system, the business records inventory purchases by debiting the inventory account; when the business makes a sale, two entries are required. The company records the sale in the usual way, debits cash or accounts receivable and credits sales revenue for the price of goods sold. The company also debits cost of goods sold and credits the cost to inventory. The charge to inventory (for purchases) serves to keep an up-to-date record of the inventory on hand. The inventory account and the cost of goods sold account carry a current balance during the period.

The periodic inventory system:

In the periodic inventory system the business does not keep a continuous record of inventory on hand, rather, at the end of the period, the business takes a physical count of the inventory on hand and applies unit costs to determine the cost of ending inventory. This is the inventory figure that appears on the Balance Sheet. It is also used to calculate the cost of goods sold. The periodic system is also known as the physical system, because it relies on the actual physical count of inventory. The periodic system is generally used to account for inventory items that have a low unit cost. Low-cost items may not be valuable enough to warrant the cost of keeping an up-to-date record of inventory on hand. To use the periodic system effectively, the owner must have the ability to control inventory by visual inspection. For example, when a customer requests certain quantities on hand, the owner or manager can view the existing stock.

INVENTORIES

Warehouse management and inventory control are knowledge and functions that every company director must know and differentiate clearly, in order to optimise the logistics operations of his company. The book highlights the importance of each activity and what their main differences are. The indiscriminate management of Warehouse Management and Inventory Control undoubtedly leads to a sub-optimisation of the operational processes of organisations, with special emphasis on those that deal with production logistics. It is therefore very important to separate inventory control management from warehousing management. The warehousing function focuses on two main aspects: One is to preserve the quality of products from the time they enter the warehouse until they leave to be used as raw materials in production or to be sold as finished goods. The second function refers to the fact of always keeping physical stocks in correspondence with the stocks recorded on cards or in electronic systems (kartdex records). In relation to inventory control, there are several inventory situations that refer to when and how inventories should be controlled. Thus, we have inventories in transit (inventories in the process of acquisition and delivery); physical inventories;

theoretical inventories; and committed inventories.

Having explained the above, it is clear that the term materials or stock in a warehouse is totally different from inventory control. For these reasons and others of greater importance, one of the objectives of this book is to explain, in the first place, how storage and inventories influence the optimisation of financial resources, which are the essence of any administration. Company managers are increasingly aware and concerned about inventories because they are investments that represent a high percentage of assets, and are paying more and more attention to their control, management, preservation and custody.

Taking into consideration the importance for any business institution of good management of consumables, spare parts, office supplies, packaging materials, raw materials and finished products, it is imperative to manage inventories according to the best practices of conservation and maintenance. Similarly, the financial indicators based on inventory turnover and the new trends of the "Just in Time" and "Total Quality" philosophies, among others, which affect the principles of finance, production, marketing and materials management in any company or institution, guide us in applying the most advanced procedures for planning, organising, directing and controlling inventories.

Carelessness in inventory management leads to three main issues that every organisation wants to avoid: Excess, Waste and Variability. Excessive inventories hide problems, lead to damage and obsolescence of materials and widen the   planning   horizon, creating greater uncertainty   .

That is why this book is presented, whose main purpose is to provide the knowledge and results that are expected in all operational areas of an organisation, through a rational and effective management of
i
nventories.

Finally, it is important to note that the book is derived from the research project of the National Polytechnic Institute, with Registration assigned by the Secretariat for Research Projects: 20141207 entitled: "The best practices of the administrative process applied to SMEs to consolidate their sustainable development and their permanence in a global scenario".

OBJECTIVES OF THE INVENTORY PLANNING AND CONTROL DEPARTMENT.

The planning and control of inventories seeks to satisfy in the foreground the objectives of the departments that are most directly related to the company's operations, such as sales, production and finance. 1. Sales Department. Objective: To provide the appropriate level of service to the sales department. 2. Production Department. Objective: To maintain the fluidity of the production processes. 3. Finance Department. Objective: To optimise inventory investment costs.

FUNCTIONS OF THE INVENTORY PLANNING AND CONTROL DEPARTMENT.

The functions of the inventory planning and control department derive from the interface between the departments mentioned in the previous point. These departments manifest conflicting interests because the sales department demands high inventories of certain products in order to provide a high level of service to customers. On the other hand, the production department requires high inventories of raw materials, in order not to stop its processes and to make production runs as large as possible. As far as the finance department is concerned, its main objective is to provide the highest possible dividend payments to shareholders, which can only be achieved if the financial structure of the company is properly managed and depends to a certain extent on average inventories, which must be kept as low as possible. Therefore, the role of the inventory planning and control department consists of: Coordinate the conflicting interests of the sales, production and finance departments to ensure that material resources are available:

A. With opportunity.
B. In the right place.

C. In the quantities required.
D. With the specifications indicated.
E. With the optimal inventory investment cost

CLASSIFICATION OF INVENTORIES ACCORDING TO THEIR NATURE.

The nature of inventories is determined by their intended use. According to this condition, inventories can be divided into: 1.- Manufacturing inventories: Raw materials - Parts, Materials in process - Assemblies and sub-assemblies. Complete finished products and spare parts. 2.- Preservation and maintenance inventories: Spare parts: Tools: Machine parts: Equipment: Lubricants: Cleaning items: Hardware items: General consumables.

Inventories of office supplies: Stationery: Printed forms, General consumables. Inventories of fixed assets: Machinery and Equipment; Furniture, Land, Buildings, Transport, others. These inventories are not consumables and are therefore controlled differently from general consumption inventories.

CLASSIFICATION OF INVENTORIES ACCORDING TO THEIR FUNCTION.

One of the most important functions of inventories is to meet the variability of demand. Variability caused by inconsistent customer demand and suppliers' failure to meet delivery times. To express this function graphically we can make the simile with the shock absorbers of a car.

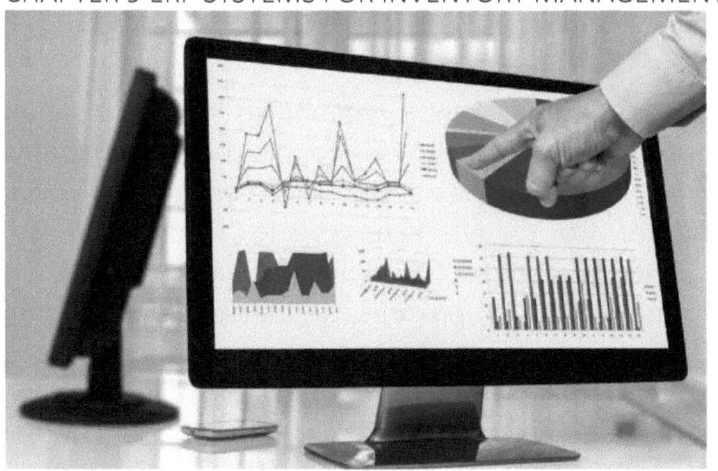

Nowadays Real-Time Inventory when talking about ERP systems is an over-understanding, as any modern system includes this function. However, even more important is the accuracy of the inventory.

We need to define: What is "Real Time Inventory" and why is it important?

When a transaction with a computer system is processed and completed in a short period of time, this is referred to as "real-time" processing. From the user's perspective, a real-time transaction is one that is completed immediately.

Real-time transaction processing is indispensable in certain industries. This is easy to understand when you think of hotel or flight bookings. But is it necessary in the inventory management of an ERP system?

In many cases the answer is a resounding "yes". Consider this simple example: a sales organisation has many customers with direct access to the sales system, either via the Internet or via private access (VPN Virtual Private Network) to the company's ERP. When a customer orders an item, the transaction is processed immediately, so the inventory is updated directly. When the next customer orders the same item the system can let the customer know precisely if there is stock of that item and if the order can be shipped. In this case, real-time inventory management provides a better experience for all involved.

Practical issues with real-time inventory management.

Needless to say, most modern ERP systems process transactions in real-time, often including accounting transactions (where there is no urgent need for real-time processing), so in a purely practical sense we could ignore the question of the "why" of real-time inventory management. In most cases the functionality is already there! However, there are practical reasons why obtaining real-time inventory information is not as simple as it seems.

To explore this issue in depth, let us concentrate on the relationship between real-time processing and the (sometimes manual) work that follows real-time transactions.

Let's say, for example, a customer orders an item online. In the confirmation process carried out by the sales module, a query will be made to the inventory module to corroborate the availability of the ordered item. There are several possible scenarios:

The ordered item is in stock: The customer will receive confirmation of the order, detailing the delivery date, price and quantity. This can be done in real time via email. The inventory module will register the sales order for this particular item and will consider it when performing other availability checks in the future.

The ordered item is not in stock: The customer must be notified and asked if he/she agrees to put it on backorder. If he agrees, the inventory module sends a replenishment order to the purchasing module. Up to this point all this is done in real time. The sourcing department then processes the purchase notification and from the perspective of the original purchase order this process did not occur in real time. .

The inventory module records (in real time) the purchased items individually and will associate them to each of the corresponding stock items. Data such as expected delivery date and quantity are important for the aforementioned availability checks.

The supplier confirms the purchase order. For the inventory module this is relevant because the confirmation is associated with the shipment date, the quantity and the price. This information is stored in the inventory at item level.

Individually purchased items are received. When this happens the inventory of the items is updated in real time.

Orders are delivered. When sold items are collected for subsequent shipment (automatically or annually), the corresponding inventory records are updated (at the same time or shortly thereafter).

The inventory management module of the ERP system produces a list of purchase notices, based on minimum stock levels and/or purchase alerts from availability checks in the sales process. When the list of purchase alerts is accepted (partially or fully), this fact can be recorded and inventories will be updated accordingly.

Completed purchase orders are received. The inventory clerk who receives the items and places them in stock can record this fact by simply accessing the purchase order and tagging it as received. The relevant inventory records are updated in real time.

All of the above is aimed at ensuring the accuracy and precision of inventory data. In this respect, accuracy of price and stock quantities is particularly important.

Let us now examine the quantity in stock. The inventory management module of the ERP software must correctly establish for each item the physical quantity that corresponds to it. In addition to the physical quantity there is a target quantity. When carrying out an availability check (see above) the quantity that is considered is the target quantity.

For example: when a customer orders 25 pieces of a particular item and the physical stock is 50, we would say that there is enough for this customer. However, if a previous customer had ordered 40 pieces then there would be a shortage of 15. There are several ways to deal with this problem that are beyond the scope of this article.

The target quantity is calculated by the ERP as follows: (physical quantity) + (quantity purchased but not yet received) - (quantity sold but not yet shipped).

When an item is shipped to the customer, the quantity delivered is subtracted from both the physical quantity and the quantity sold but not yet delivered. When an item is received from the supplier, the quantity received is added to the physical quantity and subtracted from the quantity purchased but not yet received.

This all looks simple enough, but the reality is that many companies have complications with physical stock accuracy. Often, the problem is that the physical quantities set by the ERP system do not match the physical quantities on the shelves.

Some of the possible causes:
1. Theft.
2. Occasional errors in administration, handling and storage of items.
3. Lack of consistent discipline in handling items and information. Damage to unreported items.
4. Too much time between the effective date of the printout of the cycle count list and the actual date of counting the physical quantities in stock.

Conclusion

Real-time by itself is no guarantee of precision and accuracy. Real-time processing must be accompanied by the correct execution of the corresponding manual and administrative work. Every effort must be made to ensure the accuracy of the manual and administrative work. Furthermore, the inventory must be adequately protected against theft and preventable damage.

Do you know how long your company's inventory will be stored before it is sold or when you will make a profit on those products? Do you believe that a full inventory is the recipe to keep your customers happy and bring you a lot of profit?
If you have the answer to these 2 questions, it is probably because your company does not properly manage the inventory or the information it is capable of providing us with. That is, if you manage your inventories with an ERP (Enterprise Resource Planning).

What are the benefits of managing inventory information with an ERP?

By managing your company's inventories with an ERP you will see improvements in the commercial and accounting processes, as this type of system integrates the processes that can be carried out within a business, creating a channel where information flows automatically from each area and process of the business.

Some of the many benefits you will see in your business after managing inventories with an ERP are as follows:

Control over and shortages of inventories.
You will manage stock removals.

You will generate merchandise orders automatically.
Effective tracking and management of purchases with the objective of determining the levels of expenditure managed in your company.
Improvements in the flow of goods.
Tracking of serial numbers and warehouse references.
Stock control.
Updated reports with movements, transfers and adjustments of goods made.
Sales, distribution, production and collection areas will improve their work rhythm by having updated and real information from inventories.
Ability to keep electronic accounting and therefore to comply with SAT.
Updated financial reports.

How to keep inventories with an erp?

An ERP or Resource Planning System is structured by the modules that make up a company, for example:

Accounting
Purchases

Sales
Inventories
Production

To name but a few. And its main function is to manage and control the resources, processes and operations of your business.

Having such a system in your company will not only improve inventory control, but also the rest of the areas of the company. ERPs allow you to have a better control and knowledge of each department of the business; being on the web, they manage and provide information in real time, sharing the data requested at the time you want.

One of the most important benefits of ERP systems is that they generate analysis of financial trends, which allows you to quickly obtain reports when you need them, making it easier for you to make decisions based on accurate information.

SIEP/ENTERPRISE is an ERP system to manage your company with which you will forget about problems with your inventories and will guide you in the important task of managing your business and its processes from a single place.
You'll also do your company's accounting electronically, improve business processes and comply with regulations all with a single ERP system.

BIBLIOGRAPHY

1. Operations Research. Author: Hamdy A. Taha
2. Production Planning and Control. Author: Daniel Sipper - Robert L. Bulfin Jr.
3. Production and Inventory Systems. Author: Elwood S. Buffa - William H. Taubert.
4. Production and Operations Management. Author: Norman Gaither - Greg Frazier.
5. Production Planning and Control. Author: Thomas E. Vollman - William L. Berry - D. Clay Whybark - F. Robert Jacobs

Table of contents

yes
I want morebooks!

Buy your books fast and straightforward online - at one of world's fastest growing online book stores! Environmentally sound due to Print-on-Demand technologies.

Buy your books online at
www.morebooks.shop

Kaufen Sie Ihre Bücher schnell und unkompliziert online – auf einer der am schnellsten wachsenden Buchhandelsplattformen weltweit! Dank Print-On-Demand umwelt- und ressourcenschonend produzi ert.

Bücher schneller online kaufen
www.morebooks.shop

Printed by Books on Demand GmbH, Norderstedt / Germany